Families

Family Responsibilities

Debbie Gallagher

 **Marshall Cavendish**
Benchmark
New York

This edition first published in 2009 in the United States of America by Marshall Cavendish Benchmark.

Marshall Cavendish Benchmark
99 White Plains Road
Tarrytown, NY 10591
www.marshallcavendish.us

First published in 2008 by
MACMILLAN EDUCATION AUSTRALIA PTY LTD
15–19 Claremont St, South Yarra 3141

Visit our Web site at www.macmillan.com.au or go directly to www.macmillanlibrary.com.au

Associated companies and representatives throughout the world.

Library of Congress Cataloging-in-Publication Data

Gallagher, Debbie, 1969-
    Family responsibilities / by Debbie Gallagher.
        p. cm. — (Families)
    Includes index.
    ISBN 978-0-7614-3141-1
    1. Family—Juvenile literature. 2. Responsibility—Juvenile literature. I. Title.
    HQ744.G38 2008
306.85—dc22
                                        2008001666

Edited by Georgina Garner
Text and cover design by Christine Deering
Page layout by Raul Diche
Photo research by Brendan Gallagher

Printed in the United States

Acknowledgments
The author and the publisher are grateful to the following for permission to reproduce copyright material:

Front cover photograph: Boy taking out recycling © Corbis Royalty Free

Photos courtesy of: © Zsolt Nyulaszi/123RF, **22**, © Lisa Young/123RF, **27**; AAP/Comstock, **3**, **24**; AusAID, **10**; AusAID, photo by Will Salter, **6**, **8**; Corbis Royalty Free, **1**, **17**; © Brownm39/Dreamstime.com, **29**; © Davidpark/Dreamstime.com, **23**; © Marcopolo/Dreamstime.com, **14**; The DW Stock Picture Library, **19**; © Hallgerd/Fotolia, **5**; Getty Images/Photodisc, **20**; © North Georgia Media L.L.C./iStockphoto, **26**; Photo-Easy.com, **7**, **12**, **28**; Photos.com, **21**; Pure Stock Images, **16**; Shutterstock, **15**; © Galina Barskaya/Shutterstock, **9**; © Olga Lyubkina/Shutterstock, **25**; © kristian sekulic/Shutterstock, **18**; © Vishal Shah/Shutterstock, **4**; © Nick Stubbs/Shutterstock, **11**; © Bruce Yeung/Shutterstock, **13**.

While every care has been taken to trace and acknowledge copyright, the publisher tenders their apologies for any accidental infringement where copyright has proved untraceable. Where the attempt has been unsuccessful, the publisher welcomes information that would redress the situation.

Contents

Families 4

Family Responsibilities 6

Types of Responsibilities 8

Providing Food, Shelter, and Clothing 10

Doing Jobs Around the Home 14

Looking After Each Other 18

Loving and Caring for Each Other 20

Helping Each Other 22

Teaching Each Other 24

Passing on Family Heritage 28

Your Responsibilities 30

Glossary 31

Index 32

Glossary words

When a word is printed in **bold**, you can look up its meaning in the Glossary on page 31.

Families

Families live in countries all around the world. Some of your friends may have a family just like yours. Some of your friends may have families very different from yours.

Families live together all over the world.

Each member of a family has **responsibilities**. Family members may share responsibilities or they may each take a different responsibility. Everyone has a **role** to play in the family.

A grandmother may share the responsibility for looking after her grandchildren.

Marion Public Library
1095 6th Avenue
Marion, IA 52302-3428
(319) 377-3412

Family Responsibilities

Family responsibilities are the jobs that help everyone in the family. A family works together happily when each member takes on the responsibilities of his or her role.

Collecting water is an important family responsibility in some places.

In some families, one person may work to provide food to feed the family. It is everyone's responsibility to make sure all family members feel loved.

In some families, the mother prepares grain for her family to eat.

Types of Responsibilities

Each family member has different types of responsibilities. Some responsibilities may be jobs around the home, such as washing the dishes. These jobs may be different in different **cultures**.

This Vietnamese girl is responsible for cleaning the pigpen.

It is a responsibility to be home at an agreed time. Looking after each other in the **extended family** and teaching **traditions** are also family responsibilities.

A parent teaches a child how to cut cucumber coils.

Providing Food, Shelter, and Clothing

An important family responsibility is to provide food, shelter, and clothing. In some places, families grow or catch their own food and make and mend their clothes.

This man is watering his family's vegetable garden in Cambodia.

In many families, people work to earn money to pay for food, a home, and clothing.

A man buys food for his family with money he earned working.

A Family Business

Some families have their own business, such as a shop or a **restaurant**. Often, several family members work in the business as well. Their jobs depend on their age and **skills**.

These children spend a lot of time around the family hardware store.

A family farm can provide some of the food a family needs. Animals and crops are often sold to pay for other needs, such as clothes.

Family members work together to farm their land in Nepal.

Doing Jobs Around the Home

Doing jobs around the home is another family responsibility. A home needs to be kept clean and dry.

Sometimes, repairs need to be made around the home.

Often, the work of looking after the home is shared among family members. Even young children have responsibilities. They might wash dishes, rake leaves, or take out the garbage.

Even young children can do jobs around the home.

Earning Pocket Money

Often a child's first job is done at home. A child might earn a small amount of money each week to do extra jobs for the family. This money is called pocket money.

Pocket money can help children learn about saving and spending money.

Some children feed the animals, collect eggs from the hens, or set the table for dinner.

This boy earns his pocket money by taking out the recycling.

Looking After Each Other

Family members help take care of each other's health. Making fresh, healthy meals and going for walks together are ways they help each other.

Participating in sports and doing other activities together can help keep a family healthy.

If people get sick, others in the family may
look after them.

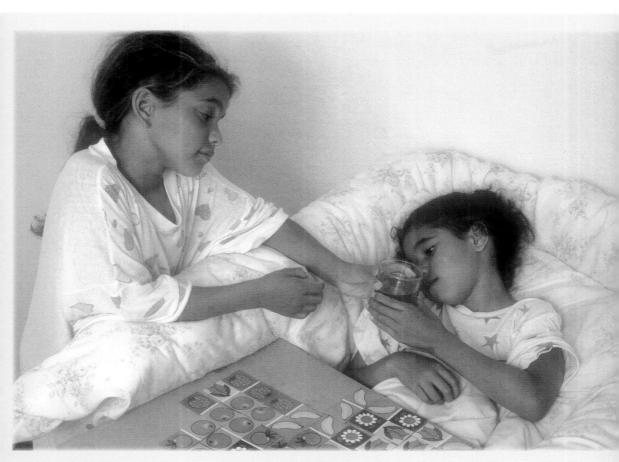

A young girl helps look after her sick sister.

Loving and Caring for Each Other

Family members are responsible for loving and caring for each other. Sisters, brothers, grandparents, and uncles give love, **respect**, support, and encouragement to each other.

Family members talk to each other about their disappointments and achievements.

Getting together with **relatives** allows families to share time and experiences. Family members who live in different countries may share ideas and difficult experiences through letters or emails.

Stories and experiences are shared over the phone.

Helping Each Other

Very young family members often need extra help from other family members. As people age, they may need help to do things they used to do themselves.

Babies need help with most things, especially eating.

Older members have a lot they can do for the family. They have learned many things in their life that they can teach younger **generations**.

Older family members often have time to talk.

Teaching Each Other

Teaching is another important responsibility for family members. Young people learn skills and lessons from older members. Many children go to school to learn things.

A parent takes responsibility for his child's education at home.

Children can also learn from the way older
family members behave or do things themselves.
Children can learn skills and values from watching
older people.

A father teaches his son to paddle a kayak.

Passing on Skills

There are many different skills families can pass on to each other. Younger family members may teach older members computer skills or a new language.

Children who learn about computers sometimes help older members of the family.

Older family members may also have skills they can teach. This might be how to drive a car, bake bread, play music, or draw.

A father teaches his daughter how to play guitar.

Passing on Family Heritage

A family has an important responsibility to pass on its **heritage**. Stories about the family's past are often told to children. This gives them a sense of their background.

Children in Bolivia are taught to play traditional music and carry on their heritage.

A family protects its heritage by practicing cultural, religious, and language traditions. These traditions give a family its identity.

A Buddhist family makes a traditional offering at a temple.

Your Responsibilities

What family responsibilities do you have? Your responsibilities might be jobs you do around the home or the things you do to earn pocket money.

Try this!

Make a list of all the ways you help take care of your family.

My Responsibilities

✔ Feed the chickens and change their water (every day)

✔ Set the dinner table (every day)

✔ Help everyone clean up after dinner (every day)

✔ Do my homework (every day)

✔ Help Granddad with the vegetable garden (every week)

✔ Visit Uncle Mike's family and Oma (every month)

✔ Do extra jobs on the farm during the holidays

✔ Write to Aunt Marine

Glossary

cultures	groups of people with the same traditions and practices
extended family	all the members of a family, not just the parents and children
generations	the groups of people in a family who are usually born around the same time and are on the same level in a family tree
heritage	things that are passed down from past family members
relatives	people who are part of your family
respect	treating someone with consideration
responsibilities	duties and things that you need to take care of
restaurant	a place where you can pay to eat a meal prepared for you
role	the position or part that a person plays in life
skills	things you can do well
traditions	beliefs, stories, or practices that have been followed by a group of people over time

Index

B
babies,   22
business,   12, 13

E
extended family,   9

F
farm,   13
food,   7, 10, 11

H
health,   18, 19
heritage,   28, 29
home,   8, 9, 11, 14, 15

J
jobs,   8, 12, 14, 15, 16, 17, 30

L
learning,   24, 25
love,   7, 20

M
money,   11, 16, 17, 30
music,   27

O
older family members,   22, 23,
    24, 25, 26, 27

P
pocket money,   16, 17, 30

R
relatives,   21
roles,   5, 6

S
sharing time,   21
skills,   12, 24, 25, 26, 27

T
teaching,   24, 25, 26, 27
traditions,   9, 29

V
values,   25

W
work,   6, 7, 10, 11, 12, 14, 15